The *Musée imaginaire* of
VAN GOGH

VINCENT'S CHOICE

VAN GOGH MUSEUM – MAROT – TIJDSBEELD

CREDITS

This publication accompanies the exhibition *Vincent's choice: the Musée imaginaire of Van Gogh*, organised by the Van Gogh Museum, Amsterdam (14 February - 15 June 2003). The installation of the exhibition was designed by Thierry W. Despont, New York.

EXHIBITION

coordination
Andreas Blühm

curators
Andreas Blühm, Sjraar van Heugten, Chris Stolwijk, with the assistance of Nienke Bakker

registrars
Martine Kilburn, Sara Verboven

secretaries
Esther Hoofwijk, Adrie Kok

lighting design
Johnson Schwinghammer Lighting, New York

exhibition installation
Iris Vormgeving, Amsterdam

graphic design
Frederik de Wal, Schelluinen

main sponsor
Rabobank

PUBLICATION

editing
Chris Stolwijk and Irene Smets, with assistance of Aukje Vergeest

with special thanks to the authors of the catalogue
Nienke Bakker, Joan Greer, Sjraar van Heugten, Cornelia Homburg, Leo Jansen, Hans Luijten, Chris Stolwijk, Evert van Uitert, Wouter van der Veen, Roelie Zwikker

production
Tijdsbeeld, Ghent, Ronny Gobyn (director), assisted by Petra Gunst and Barbara Costermans (Tijdgeest, Ghent)

copy editing
Michael Reaburn

translation
Rachel Esner

manager of publications Van Gogh Museum
Suzanne Bogman

design
Kris Demey, Ghent

colour separations and printing
Die Keure, Bruges

photography
All photographs are courtesy of the institutions or persons owning the work reproduced. With special thanks to: Cussac/Speltdoorn: 16-1; Frédéric Jaulmes: 34-1/2; Thijs Quispel: 16-2, 31-1; Réunion des Musées Nationaux: 9-1, 12-2, 17-3, 17-4, 22-1, 29-3, 30-3, 36-1; Washington, National Gallery of Art (Board of Trustees): 17-5

front cover
Vincent van Gogh, *Small pear tree in blossom*, 1888

back cover
Rembrandt van Rijn, *Self-portrait*, 1669
Vincent van Gogh, *Self-portrait as an artist*, 1888
Vincent van Gogh, *The sower with setting sun*, 1888
Jean-François Millet, *The sower*, 1850

© 2003 Van Gogh Museum, Amsterdam
© 2003 Marot, Brussels / Tijdsbeeld, Ghent
D/2003/9044/11
ISBN 2-930117-21-4

Distributed in Belgium, exclusively by Altera Diffusion, www.altera.opya.be
Distributed in the Netherlands, exclusively by Amsterdam University Press, www.aup.nl

The *Musée imaginaire* of
VAN GOGH

FOREWORD

Vincent van Gogh (1853-1890)

Self-portrait as an artist, 1888, Amsterdam,

Van Gogh Museum (Vincent van Gogh Foundation)

Vincent van Gogh was born on 30 March 1853 – exactly 150 years ago in 2003. To celebrate this occasion, the Van Gogh Museum has organised a number of special events and activities in honour of this extraordinary painter. The exhibition *Vincent's choice: the Musée imaginaire of Van Gogh* plays a central role in these festivities. Its subject is Van Gogh's taste in art and literature: what he liked and disliked, what stimulated and influenced him. In addition to his well-known sources of inspiration – Delacroix, Gauguin, Millet, Rembrandt, the School of Barbizon, the impressionists and Japanese prints – a whole range of hitherto unknown aspects of the artist's interests will be explored, creating, in effect, a complete *musée imaginaire*.

Few artists have written as extensively and with so much insight on art and literature as Vincent van Gogh. His letters allow us to trace the progress of his taste – from his youthful observations as an art dealer, to his time as a painter at the forefront of the Parisian avant-garde, and the eager reflections of his last months. The evolution of Van Gogh's preferences cannot be separated from the development of his art, and the exhibition seeks to clarify this connection.

The present publication offers the broader public a chance to become better acquainted with Vincent van Gogh's taste.

VAN GOGH'S LIFE AND WORK: A BRIEF CHRONOLOGY

1853

30 March: Vincent Willem van Gogh is born in Zundert. He is the eldest son of the Reverend Theodorus van Gogh (1822-1885) and Anna Cornelia Carbentus (1819-1907).

1857

1 May: birth of his brother Theo.

1861-68

Schooling in Zundert, Zevenbergen and Tilburg.

1869-76

– 30 July 1869: enters the employment of the international art dealers Goupil & Cie in The Hague.
– September 1872: start of his (surviving) correspondence with Theo.
– 1 January 1873: Theo, too, takes a post with Goupil & Cie, at the Brussels branch.
– In 1873 Vincent is transferred to the firm's London office, where he remains – with the exception of three months spent in Paris – until 15 May 1875. He is then moved to the French capital. Having been dismissed from his position at Goupil's, he returns to his parents' house in Etten in 1876.

1876-80

Works as a teacher in England and, later, in a bookshop in the Netherlands; studies to become a preacher in Amsterdam and Laken (Brussels), and in 1878 goes to the Borinage mining district (southern Belgium) as an evangelist. In August 1880 decides to become an artist. His role model is the peasant painter Jean-François Millet.

1881

Stays in Brussels and then with his parents in Etten. Pre-Christmas visit to The Hague to study with his relative, the painter Anton Mauve. Following an altercation with his family around Christmas he returns to The Hague. Produces his first watercolours and painted still lifes. Begins receiving an allowance from Theo.

1882

Takes painting and drawing lessons with Mauve, but soon falls out with him as well.

1883

In September leaves The Hague for the province of Drenthe. Suffers under poor working conditions, a lack of funds and isolation. In December returns to his parents in Nuenen.

1884

Rents a studio near his parents' house and later moves there; gives painting lessons to several amateur artists.

1885

Reverend Van Gogh dies at the end of March. In late April Vincent finishes his first masterpiece, *The potato eaters*. Paints a large number of still lifes, studies of heads, and landscapes. A visit to the Rijksmuseum in Amsterdam proves a great source of inspiration (Rembrandt, Hals). Moves to Antwerp in November. Is particularly

Vincent van Gogh (1853-1890)
The painter on the road to Tarascon, 1888, destroyed
(formerly Magdeburg, Kaiser Friedrich Museum)

Vincent van Gogh, *The yellow house ('The street')*, 1888,
Amsterdam, Van Gogh Museum
(Vincent van Gogh Foundation)

Vincent van Gogh (1853-1890), *Self-portrait dedicated to Paul Gauguin (Bonze)*, 1888, Cambridge MA,
Fogg Art Museum, Harvard University Art Museums
Bequest – Collection of Maurice Wertheim, Class of 190⬤

impressed by Rubens's palette and brushwork, and discovers Japanese prints.

1886

Registers at the Antwerp art academy but soon becomes embroiled in a conflict about his manner of drawing. Leaves to join his brother Theo in Paris, where he works for several months in the studio of Fernand Cormon and becomes acquainted with the work of the impressionists and the younger avant-garde. Increasing appreciation of the work of Delacroix, Puvis de Chavannes and Adolphe Monticelli.

1887

The influence of Japanese prints on his art grows. Works in the spring with Paul Signac in the Paris suburb of Asnières. Paints portraits, city views, landscapes in a neo-impressionist style and organises an exhibition of works by his friends in the avant-garde, whom he dubs 'the impressionists of the Petit Boulevard'.

1888

Moves to Arles. Paints a series of blossoming fruit trees, several seascapes with fishing boats at Saintes-Maries-de-la-Mer, sowers, still lifes,

wheat fields, portraits, autumn gardens and night scenes. In October Paul Gauguin arrives to work with him at the Yellow House. Following a serious dispute at the end of December, in the course of which Vincent cuts off a piece of his earlobe, Gauguin leaves Arles for Paris.

1889

Paints, among other subjects, sunflowers, a self-portrait and a portrait of Madame Roulin. At the end of April commits himself to the asylum of Saint-Paul-de-Mausole at Saint-Rémy. Is given a studio and paints in the institution's garden and nearby surroundings, depicting flowers, wheat fields, olive trees and cypresses. Suffers a number of attacks of mental illness. As in 1888, however, he participates in the Salon des Indépendants in Paris.

1890

Exhibits five paintings with the artists' group Les Vingt in Brussels; one painting is sold. Represented with ten works (chosen by Theo) at the Salon des Indépendants in Paris. Leaves the asylum in May. Travels to Paris to see Theo and then on to the rural town of Auvers-sur-Oise, where he enters the care of Dr Paul Gachet. Paints, among other subjects, the wheat fields in the neighbourhood. On 27 July shoots himself in the chest. Dies of his wounds on 29 July, with Theo at his side.

Vincent van Gogh (1853-1890)
The garden of Saint Paul's Hospital, 1889, Amsterdam,
Van Gogh Museum (Vincent van Gogh Foundation)

YOUTH

Vincent van Gogh (1853-1890)
The old church tower at Nuenen, 'The peasants' churchyard', 1885,
Amsterdam, Van Gogh Museum (Vincent van Gogh Foundation)

Vincent van Gogh (1853-1890)
Recollection of Brabant, 1890, Amsterdam,
Van Gogh Museum (Vincent van Gogh Foundation)

Van Gogh's youth was spent educating himself and searching for a goal in life – at least, that is, until 1880, when he finally decided to become an artist. What were his thoughts on art in these years? What aroused his admiration?

Even as a boy, Van Gogh had a great love of art and literature. As the son of a minister, his upbringing was naturally deeply religious. In his home environment, pictures and books played an important pedagogical role. Cultural artefacts were valued above all for their ethical function: they might also be beautiful, but their main aim was to convey a moral or religious message. In his early years, then, Van Gogh was particularly attracted to works on pious themes, such as those by Ary Scheffer. Two of Van Gogh's uncles were important art dealers, and from a young age both Vincent and Theo were well acquainted with the world of art, encouraging each other in their aesthetic explorations. Vincent was an avid reader – both of novels and (art) historical literature – and he built up a large collection of prints and reproductions. He was drawn to a wide variety of styles and subject matter. He admired the work of the artists of the Hague School, such as Israëls, Maris and Weissenbruch; the Barbizon painters, among them Jules Dupré, Corot and Daubigny; and the 17th-century Dutch masters.

Van Gogh's determination to absorb all this diverse material was prompted in large part by a constant need for development and self-improvement. In the period 1869-80 he envisaged his life more or less along the lines set out by his parents, who hoped to see him climb the social ladder and attain a position as a respectable member of society, either as an art dealer or, like his father, as a clergyman. As yet, Christian values determined his choices.

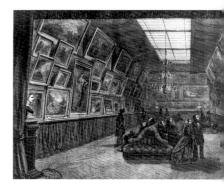

Gallery of Goupil & Cie
in the rue Chaptal, Paris, c. 1860

Johan Hendrik Weissenbruch (1824-1903)
View of the Trekvliet, 1870,
The Hague, Gemeentemuseum

Matthijs Maris (1839-1917)
The Nieuwe Haarlemse Sluis on the Singel,
called 'Souvenir d'Amsterdam', 1871,
Amsterdam, Rijksmuseum

In 1869 Van Gogh became a junior apprentice at Goupil & Cie, an internationally renowned firm of art dealers. Between 1869 and 1876 he worked successively in The Hague, London and Paris. He came into daily contact with works of contemporary art and had the opportunity to visit many museums and private collections. New names were added to his list of favourite artists, among them Charles De Groux and Jean-François Millet, who would maintain an important place in his artistic pantheon throughout his career.

In 1876 Van Gogh quit his post as an art dealer and left Paris. He then worked at a number of jobs in various places, none of them for very long. He moved to Amsterdam to prepare for studies in theology, but eventually abandoned the plan. Motivated by religious idealism, he travelled to the Borinage district of Belgium, where as a lay preacher he hoped to improve the lives of the impoverished miners. At this period he read (among other works) *Uncle Tom's cabin* (1852) by Harriet Beecher Stowe and Charles Dickens's *Hard times* (1854), novels that reinforced his image of the labourer as hard-working and courageous. These authors were highly critical of the widespread exploitation of the poor and preached a Christian message of charity that greatly appealed to him. Little changed in either Van Gogh's cultural understanding or his taste in the years 1876-80; he was, however, drifting further and further away from the path set out for him by his family.

In 1880 he suddenly, and unexpectedly, resolved to become an artist. One of the reasons for his decision was a deep-felt yearning for what he called the imaginary 'land of pictures'. If previously he had hoped to bring enlightenment and consolation to the needy through faith, he now regarded art as the best means of achieving his goal. He placed his need for intellectual and artistic sustenance almost entirely in the service of a desire to become an artist with a personal style.

RELIGION

Ary Scheffer (1795-1858), *Christus consolator*, 1837,
Amsterdams Historisch Museum (on loan to the Van Gogh Museum, Amsterdam)

Vincent van Gogh (1853-1890)
Still life with Bible, 1885,
Amsterdam, Van Gogh Museum
(Vincent van Gogh Foundation)

In the rural vicarage where Vincent spent his youth, Christian values were the order of the day, and they had a powerful formative influence on him. His father, Reverend Theodorus van Gogh, subscribed to a rather moderate form of Protestantism and was a follower of the so-called Groningen School, whose adherents believed dogma was less important than the practice of Christian charity. God was revealed not only in the Word but also in creation, and thus in both human beings and the natural world. The figure of Christ played an important role in this more evangelical and individualistic conception of faith. His example of humility, service to others and solidarity with the oppressed was to serve as a model for all those wishing to lead a virtuous life. He was also viewed as the saviour and consoler of the poor and infirm, and this undoubtedly helps explain the enormous popularity of Ary Scheffer's *Christus consolator* in devout circles of the time.

For many years, Van Gogh sought and found consolation in the faith in which he had been raised. Religious and social motifs in paintings and prints appealed to him precisely because they answered to this particular need. Following his involuntary transfer to the Paris branch of Goupil & Cie in 1875, he became obsessed with religion. He regarded his father as a role model, took the doctrinal views of his youth to new extremes, filled his letters with edifying texts, and decorated his room with numerous pious images, among them the *Christus consolator*, his favourite print. After failing to become a minister, his convictions led him to try and help the miners in the Borinage, not only by bringing them the word of God but also by personally looking after the destitute and sick among them, in 'imitation of Christ'. This all-consuming religious fervour continued to grow in the years up to 1880 and was accompanied by enormous mental strain.

Finally, in August 1880, Van Gogh made a radical decision: from this point onwards he would devote himself solely to art. The end of the Borinage period brought with it a definitive rupture with the church and its representatives. In future, Van Gogh would repudiate all forms of dogmatism. This did not, however, mean that he rejected Christianity as a whole: the humanistic and charitable spirit of the gospel continued

Emile Bernard (1868-1941)
The road to Calvary, 1889,
private collection

Vincent van Gogh (1853-1890), *Olive grove*, 1889,
Amsterdam, Van Gogh Museum
(Vincent van Gogh Foundation)

to inspire him, although traditional belief and its institutions no longer provided consolation. Van Gogh stated the aim of his art in a letter to his brother Theo: 'In my pictures I want to say something consoling, like music. I want to paint men and women with something of the eternal, whose symbol used to be the halo, and that we try to achieve through radiance itself, through the vibrancy of our colouring.'

NATURE

Jacob van Ruisdael (1628/29-1682)
Dune landscape near Haarlem (Le buisson),
1647-50, Paris, Musée du Louvre

Vincent van Gogh (1853-1890)
Pollard willow, 1882,
present whereabouts unknown

Van Gogh was a great nature enthusiast. His own work and his admiration for landscape painting bear witness to a genuine feeling for the natural world, in which observation, childhood memories, love of the outdoors, nostalgia and religion all played a role.

Van Gogh was fond of many different kinds of landscapes: those of the Hague School, the School of Barbizon, 17th-century Dutch artists (such as Jan van Goyen and Jacob van Ruisdael), Constable, Monticelli, Japanese printmakers and the impressionists and post-impressionists. For a long period, the overall atmosphere or 'effect' of a work, and what he termed its 'sentiment', dictated his preferences, and he felt particularly drawn to those painters he deemed to have a personal and probing vision of their surroundings. Pictures by the landscape painters he admired – and there were many – continually led him to new associations and reminiscences.

Van Gogh's intense love of nature (and therefore also his love of landscape painting) was rooted in his childhood in Zundert, a rural community near the Dutch-Belgian border. The village was surrounded by farmland given over to rye, potatoes and oats, and by unspoiled moorland, marshes and pine forests. From an early age, Vincent went on long walks in this countryside, occasionally accompanied by his father or brother. He heard the 'larks singing above the black fields with the young green corn,' and admired 'the sparkling blue sky with the white clouds above.' Here he acquired his lifelong passion for the countryside and nature: 'everything there speaks a distinct language, everything is firm, everything explains itself.' The landscapes of his youth and first years as an artist would always remain 'inexpressibly dear' to him. As noted above, this reverence for God's creation was very much part of the Groningen School philosophy that had such an important impact on Van Gogh's early education.

Whenever he got the chance, even in later life, he would go out to the countryside to refresh himself or to look for suitable subjects to paint. According to Van Gogh, an artist could only truly observe nature and discover its 'truths' if he himself were a nature lover. An artist, he felt, should live and work in a rural environment.

Vincent van Gogh (1853-1890)

The harvest, 1888, Amsterdam, Van Gogh Museum

(Vincent van Gogh Foundation)

Jacob van Ruisdael (1628/29-1682)
View of Haarlem with bleaching grounds, The Hague,
Royal Cabinet of Paintings Mauritshuis

Claude Monet (1840-1926)
Under the pine trees at the end of the day, 1888,
Philadelphia Museum of Art, Gift of Mrs F. Otto Haas

Georges Michel (1763-1843)
Three windmills, The Hague,
Museum Mesdag

His attitude to the city, on the other hand, was decidedly ambivalent. Although he described himself as an outdoor man, he also felt drawn to the metropolis, the 'land of pictures'. He was dependent on the urban context – not only for contact with other artists, but also for the promotion and sale of his work. It was thus a comforting thought that he could regain his feeling for nature by spending time in city parks and gardens.

When in 1888 he left Paris for the south, taking with him the lessons of the impressionists and post-impressionists, Van Gogh had enormous expectations regarding the colours, light and motifs he would encounter in Provence. Capturing the southern landscape in colour became his goal. Colour was to be an autonomous, symbolically laden means of expression, the reflection of his own experience of the natural world.

In May 1890 Van Gogh moved back north. He settled in Auvers-sur-Oise, where he planned to devote himself to the 'study of peasants and landscapes from nature'. He worked at a feverish pace, and in the last months of his life painted a number of monumental, spacious landscapes with a bright palette.

During the ten years of his career as an artist, Van Gogh's thought evolved from a realistic to a more symbolic conception of art; colour became the supreme means of expression for capturing the essence of a landscape, although reality always remained his starting point. Many older and contemporary masters accompanied him on this journey, albeit at a distance. His personal vision of nature and his depiction of the world in a vibrant, glowing and contrasting range of colours have given him a unique place in the tradition of landscape painting.

PEASANT LIFE AND LABOUR

Vincent van Gogh (1853-1890)
The potato eaters, 1885, Amsterdam,
Van Gogh Museum (Vincent van Gogh Foundation)

Charles De Groux (1825-1870)
Grace, 1861, Brussels, Musées royaux
des Beaux-Arts de Belgique

One of the most striking aspects of Vincent van Gogh's taste was his life-long interest in the subjects of work and peasant life. In his own paintings and drawings, too, working men and women play a seminal role, particularly in his Dutch period (1880-85). In his first large-scale figure painting, *The potato eaters*, he sought to express the very essence of rural existence through the image of the primitive farm labourer who earns his living by the sweat of his brow.

Van Gogh's vision of the countryside and peasant life was largely determined by the fact that he grew up in a region where farming was highly respected and farmers were seen as hard-working and honest. The endemic poverty and unemployment that surrounded him were also influential. Gradually, Vincent's conception of peasants and artisans would also become coloured by art and literature. During his time in Holland, he viewed them as pious, nobly toiling men and women like those found in the paintings of Jean-François Millet and Jules Breton; Jozef Israëls's images of devout fishermen and rural labourers conformed to this concept as well. Later, he got to know the more

social-realist pictures of Charles De Groux, which depict the difficult circumstances of life among the poor in unambiguous terms.

Influenced by the naturalist novels of Emile Zola and the Goncourts, Van Gogh began to develop an interest in the coarser and more primitive aspects of the lower classes, and this new trope became mixed with the idealised image à la Millet. The painter and lithographer Honoré Daumier, as well as writers like Flaubert, Balzac and Maupassant, helped confirm his taste for the realistic approach to the human condition. In addition, his collection of prints from English and French magazines not only provided him with an insight into the methods and techniques of printmaking, but also supplied him with an arsenal of examples for the depiction of city life and figures at work, as well as accurate depictions of all the lowest strata of society. Although he was also drawn to illustrations of more socially engaged subjects, like strikes or factory workers, in his own art he focused on traditional manual labour, particularly that of the peasants. 'Painting peasant life is a serious business, and I for one would blame myself if I didn't try to make pictures that could

Constantin Meunier (1831-1905)

The return of the miners, c. 1885, private collection

Vincent van Gogh (1853-1890),
Miners, 1880, Otterlo,
Kröller-Müller Museum

Jules Breton (1827-1906),
Evening, 1860, Paris, Musée d'Orsay
(on loan to the Hôtel de Ville, Cuisery)

Jean-François Millet (1814-1875)
The gleaners, 1857,
Paris, Musée d'Orsay

give rise to serious reflection in those who think seriously about art and life. Millet, Degroux, so many others, have set an example of *character* by turning a deaf ear to such taunts as "sâle, grossier, boueux, puant" [nasty, crude, filthy, stinking] etc., etc., so it would be a disgrace should one so much as waver. No, one must paint peasants as if one were one of them, as if one felt and thought as they do.'

Vincent van Gogh (1853-1890)
Women picking olives, 1889,
Washington, National Gallery of Art,
Chester Dale Collection

JEAN-FRANÇOIS MILLET

Jean-François Millet (1814-1875), *The sower*, 1850,
Boston, Museum of Fine Arts, Gift of Quincy Adams Shaw
through Quincy Adams Shaw, Jr., and Mrs. Marian Shaw Haughton

Vincent van Gogh (1853-1890)
The sower with setting sun, 1888, Amsterdam,
Van Gogh Museum (Vincent van Gogh Foundation)

It was while working at Goupil & Cie in the early 1870s that Van Gogh discovered the art of Millet, Breton and other romantic-realist painters of rural life. He was deeply impressed with their work and as the years went by his admiration only grew – especially after reading Alfred Sensier's *La vie et l'œuvre de J.-F. Millet* (1881) in 1882. This biography presents Millet as a deeply religious man, who himself led the life of a poor peasant and never received the recognition he deserved during his lifetime. This image was only partially true, but for Van Gogh it was reason enough to declare the French painter his role model, in both art and life. He recognised in Millet a kindred spirit and used him to justify and support his decision to make 'the people' the subject of his art. Sensier's work also influenced his ideas about painting. Inspired by the author's

reference to Théophile Gautier's pronouncement that Millet's *Sower* 'appeared to be painted with the earth being sown,' Van Gogh began depicting his Nuenen peasants using thickly applied brushstrokes with a palette of earthen tones.

Van Gogh saw in the work of Millet (and Breton) an expression of religious feeling, of belief in what he called 'quelque chose là-haut' ('something up above'). He regarded the sower and the corn sheaf as symbols of the infinite and Millet's *Sower* – in which there was 'more soul than in an ordinary sower in the field' – as the apex of art. He remained fascinated with this picture throughout his life, and he made numerous painted and drawn variations on the theme.

Even after Van Gogh had become acquainted with modern French painting, Millet retained his position in the artist's pantheon. For example, he associated his own portrait of the Provençal farmhand Patience Escalier, painted in Arles, with a picture by Millet: he characterised Escalier as 'a "man with the hoe"-type' – an allusion to Millet's *Man with a hoe*, one of his so-called 'rough' paintings. While in Saint-Rémy he

Vincent van Gogh (1853-1890)
Portrait of Patience Escalier, 1888,
private collection

Jean-François Millet (1814-1875)
Man with a hoe, 1860-62,
Los Angeles, The J. Paul Getty Museum

Jean-François Millet (1814-1875)
Vineyard labourer resting, 1869-70,
The Hague, Museum Mesdag

Jean-François Millet (1814-1875)

Shearing sheep, c. 1860,

private collection

Vincent van Gogh (1853-1890)

The sheep shearer (after Millet), 1889,

Amsterdam, Van Gogh Museum

(Vincent van Gogh Foundation)

Jean-François Millet (1814-1875)

The angelus, 1857-59,

Paris, Musée d'Orsay

painted 'interpretations in colour' of Millet's *Labours of the fields*, *The sower*, *Men digging* and *The four times of the day*. In these works, he combined the latter's figures with the palette of Eugène Delacroix and the impressionists. For Van Gogh, Jean-François Millet embodied the oneness of man and nature, represented by the peasant working in the field.

Vincent van Gogh (1853-1890)

Night (after Millet), 1889,

Amsterdam, Van Gogh Museum

(Vincent van Gogh Foundation)

SENTIMENT

Pierre Puvis de Chavannes (1824-1898)
Hope, c. 1872, Paris, Musée d'Orsay

Camille Corot (1796-1875)
Sunrise, c. 1870-72,
The Hague, Museum Mesdag

Van Gogh aspired to a form of personal expression in which the exact depiction of nature or the sitter was subordinate to something he referred to as 'beyond the paint'. He viewed technique and the aesthetic as mere means in the service of the higher goal of art, namely to offer consolation, writing: '[...] we are here to comfort and to prepare the way for a more consoling kind of painting.' To derive and provide consolation – this was one of the most powerful driving forces behind Van Gogh's art. What appealed to him in paintings by his favourite masters was likewise that which lay 'beyond the paint'. For Van Gogh, the most valuable thing a book or artwork could impart was a (supposed) sense of consolation. He also prized what he called a work's 'sentiment'. This term is used repeatedly in the correspondence – something can 'be done with sentiment' or the modern artist must 'have sentiment when he paints' – and alludes to the emotion an artist could express with his work or arouse in the viewer. The subject matter contributed to this, as did the calculated use of colour, line, composition and style. The means were important, but only resulted in a successful canvas if the artist

Jozef Israëls (1824-1911), *Old friends*, 1882, Philadelphia Museum of Art,
The William L. Elkins Collection

worked with feeling and managed to create a certain mood or 'effect'.
The consolation derived from this was of a different order and was
linked to the viewer's own needs. Significant in this context is Van Gogh's
lament in a letter to Paul Gauguin: 'an art that offers consolation for
broken hearts! There are only a few who can feel it, such as you and I!!!'

REMBRANDT

Workshop of Rembrandt van Rijn (1606-1669)
The lamentation of Christ, c. 1650,
Sarasota, The John and Mable Ringling Museum of Art,
State Art Museum of Florida, Bequest of John Ringling

right:
Vincent van Gogh (1853-1890)
Self-portrait as an artist, 1888,
Amsterdam, Van Gogh Museum
(Vincent van Gogh Foundation)

Rembrandt van Rijn (1606-1669)
Self-portrait, 1669,
London, The National Gallery

Rembrandt van Rijn (1606-1669)
The Jewish bride, c. 1666,
Amsterdam, Rijksmuseum

'I am thinking more about Rembrandt than might appear from my studies,' wrote Van Gogh in November 1888. He had already become familiar with the work of this great Golden Age painter in his early youth. While in London in 1875 he saw his *Lamentation of Christ* (now attributed to the artist's workshop): 'There's a nice exhibition of old art here, including a large "Descent from the Cross" by Rembrandt, five large figures at twilight, you can imagine the emotion.' A short time later, in Paris, he saw the *The pilgrims at Emmaus*, among other paintings. In the Trippenhuis (later Rijksmuseum) in Amsterdam he delighted in *The syndics of the drapers' guild* – for him 'the most beautiful Rembrandt' – *The night watch* and *The Jewish bride*. According to Van Gogh, in the last of these Rembrandt revealed himself to be a true 'poet, that is to say Creator.' 'What a noble sentiment, infinitely deep,' he sighed.

In terms of technique, he was particularly drawn to the way Rembrandt, like Frans Hals, captured and reproduced the very essence of a subject. Colour and form were one, details served the overall effect, and a rapid working method breathed 'life' into the painting. 'What especially struck

Vincent van Gogh (1853-1890)
Portrait of Doctor Gachet, 1890,
private collection

Workshop of Rembrandt van Rijn (1606-1669)

The holy family at night, 1638-40,

Amsterdam, Rijksmuseum

Vincent van Gogh (1853-1890)

The raising of Lazarus (after Rembrandt), 1890,

Amsterdam, Van Gogh Museum (Vincent van Gogh Foundation)

me on seeing the old Dutch paintings again is that *most* of them *were painted quickly*,' he wrote in 1885. 'I have especially admired the hands by Rembrandt and Hals – hands that lived, but were *not finished* [...]. And heads too – eyes, nose, mouth done with the first brushstrokes, without any retouching whatever.' Seeking to emulate the Dutch master, he aimed to 'exaggerate the essential and purposely leave the incidentals vague.' He was impressed by the famous self-portrait in which Rembrandt depicted himself in a direct, simple and unidealised fashion, as 'old, toothless, [and] wrinkled', and he created his own *Self-portrait as an artist* in the spirit of this extraordinary masterpiece.

Van Gogh believed portraiture had an important role in modern art. He himself hoped to contribute to the revival of the genre, and he made Rembrandt – the 'great and universal, master portrait painter of the Dutch Republic' – his role model. By combining the observation of reality with his unique powers of imagination, Rembrandt had succeeded in giving everyday reality a deeper significance. Moreover, the 19th-century viewer could recognise himself or herself in his figures, despite the fact that they had been painted 200 years earlier. For Van Gogh, Rembrandt's portraits were 'more than nature, something of a revelation.' He set himself a similar goal: he wanted to take the real as his starting point, but also add something distinctive to it, so that one would be able to see the thoughts, the 'soul', of the sitter in his likeness. Van Gogh sought to achieve this above all with colour. In 1890 he executed his *Portrait of Dr Gachet*. Following in Rembrandt's footsteps, he hoped 'to paint portraits which would appear after a century to people living then as revelations.'

TEACHERS

Anton Mauve (1838-1888)
Fishing boat on the beach, 1882, The Hague,
Gemeentemuseum

Vincent van Gogh (1853-1890)
Pink peach trees, 'Souvenir de Mauve', 1888,
Otterlo, Kröller-Müller Museum

Van Gogh only decided to become an artist at the age of 27, and unlike most of his contemporaries, who had been trained at an academy or in an artist's studio, he was self-taught. He needed guidance and sought it avidly. He had many teachers. He was acquainted with some of them personally, but more often than not the most important were those he referred to as his 'paper tutors', whom he knew solely through the books written about them or their works (sometimes in the form of reproductions). His friendships with fellow-artists also contributed greatly to his development.

In 1881 he took lessons from the Hague School painter Anton Mauve, whom he admired as 'a great interpreter of [...] delicate, grey Dutch nature' and as an artist who gave 'significance' to an otherwise banal subject – as, for example, in his *Fishing boat on the beach*. After only a brief period, however, the artists parted company. Still, Van Gogh continued to speak with deep respect of 'the excellent Mauve', and in 1888 painted *Pink peach trees, 'Souvenir de Mauve'* in memory of his recently deceased master. From the autumn of 1883 to the end of 1885 Vincent

Vincent van Gogh (1853-1890)
Digger in a potato field: February, 1885,
Amsterdam, Van Gogh Museum
(Vincent van Gogh Foundation)

painted and drew successively in Drenthe and Nuenen, where he recorded the rural surroundings and worked intensively from the live model, as Mauve had advised. He focused himself on his studies with the aid of books, but without the inspirational, personal supervision of a more experienced artist.

Having spent a short time at the academy in Antwerp in early 1886, Van Gogh departed for Paris at the end of February. Determined to

Henri de Toulouse-Lautrec (1864-1901)
Mademoiselle Dihau playing the piano, 1890,
Albi, Musée Toulouse-Lautrec

Vincent van Gogh (1853-1890)
Augustine Roulin ('La berceuse'), 1888-89,
Amsterdam, Stedelijk Museum
(on loan to the Van Gogh Museum, Amsterdam)

Emile Bernard (1868-1941), *Portrait of Bernard's grandmother*, 1887, Amsterdam, Van Gogh Museum
(Vincent van Gogh Foundation)

Fernand Cormon (1845-1924)
Cain, 1880,
Paris, Musée d'Orsay

focus on the study of the human figure, he enrolled in the studio of the history painter Fernand Cormon. Here he met the young artists Henri de Toulouse-Lautrec and Emile Bernard, future members of the avant-garde. Cormon's more or less academic approach failed to satisfy him, however, and after only three months he decided he had had enough. Never again would he seek out a studio or academy, as he was convinced that no institution could teach him to paint the realities of everyday life: 'Nothing seems simpler than painting peasants or ragpickers and other workers, but – there are no subjects in painting as difficult as those everyday figures! As far as I know, there is not a single academy in which one can learn to draw and paint a digger, a sower, a woman hanging a pot over the fire, or a seamstress. But every city of any importance has an academy with a choice of models for historical, Arabic, Louis XV and, in a nutshell, every sort of figure, provided they do not exist in reality.'

Even after leaving Paris for the south of France in February 1888, Van Gogh continued to yearn for instruction and to improve himself. At the end of October, Gauguin arrived in Arles. For two months he and Vincent worked together in the Yellow House, their 'studio of the south' – a collaboration of enormous consequence in Van Gogh's search for a personal style. Gauguin was a tremendous encouragement, inspiring him to artistic experimentation; at the same time, Gauguin himself could not help but be influenced by his younger friend. In December, however, a dramatic rupture occurred. From this point onwards, Van Gogh would distance himself more and more from Gauguin's conception of art, although he would always maintain a great respect for him.

Van Gogh became acquainted with many of his teachers simply by looking at their art, collecting reproductions of their works, and reading about them in books. He had a decided preference for artists who he felt worked with love, with 'the soul', such as the Japanese printmakers. Simply having perfectly mastered a technique was not good enough: 'if there is life and feeling in it, then it is good.' Of all the painters to have exercised an influence on Van Gogh's artistic development, three played a pivotal role: Delacroix, Millet and Rembrandt, artists whose works he also copied.

Vincent van Gogh (1853-1890)

Gauguin's chair, 1888, Amsterdam,

Van Gogh Museum (Vincent van Gogh Foundation)

After Léon Lhermitte (1844-1925)
Rural labours. November: the sower, Amsterdam,
Van Gogh Museum (Vincent van Gogh Foundation)

Vincent van Gogh (1853-1890)
Torso of Venus, 1887, Amsterdam,
Van Gogh Museum (Vincent van Gogh Foundation)

Pierre Puvis de Chavannes (1824-1898)
Portrait of Eugène Benon, 1882,
private collection

Van Gogh was an avid print collector: 'When I can't sleep at night, which is quite often the case, I can always pleasurably pass the time rummaging among my woodcuts.' Regarding his illustrations from *The Graphic*, he wrote: 'In my opinion, sheets like these are a kind of Bible for the artist, which he can consult at will in order to tune himself – it is not only a good idea to know them, but to have them always about the studio.'

Nevertheless, Van Gogh's various 'teachers' were only partially responsible for the direction his art would eventually take. Equally important were the surroundings in which he worked and the contacts he made. Without such personal encounters he would never have become a truly modern painter.

VISIT TO THE RIJKSMUSEUM, AMSTERDAM

Philips Koninck (1619-1688), *River landscape*, 1676,
Amsterdam, Rijksmuseum

Copy after Frans Hals (1581/5-1666)
The fool, Amsterdam, Rijksmuseum

Having already been to its predecessor, the Trippenhuis, Van Gogh paid a visit in October 1885 to Amsterdam's recently opened Rijksmuseum. He was particularly impressed by the works of Frans Hals and Rembrandt, and his admiration for 17th-century Dutch painting was stimulated anew. He was fascinated by Hals's use of colour, calling him 'the colourist among the colourists'. Back in Nuenen, where until his departure for Antwerp at the end of November he painted mainly landscapes, he began working with a brighter palette. This resulted, among other paintings, in two views of the autumn countryside.

The visit to Amsterdam was not only important in terms of Van Gogh's use of colour; it also provided him with new insights into various aspects of portrait and figure painting, and encouraged him to experiment with a looser brush.

Jan van Goyen (1596-1656), *Landscape with two oaks*, 1641, Amsterdam, Rijksmuseum

Vincent van Gogh (1853-1890)

Lane with poplars, 1885,

Rotterdam, Museum Boijmans Van Beuningen

VISIT TO THE MUSÉE FABRE, MONTPELLIER

Eugène Delacroix (1798-1863)

Portrait of Alfred Bruyas, 1853, Montpellier, Musée Fabre

Gustave Courbet (1819-1877)

The sleeping spinner, 1853

Montpellier, Musée Fabre

The art-theoretical discussions in which Van Gogh and Gauguin engaged in Arles at the end of 1888 only confirmed Vincent's long-standing preference for artists such as Daumier, Delacroix, Millet, Puvis de Chavannes and Rembrandt. He remained committed to the notion that the in-depth study of nature was a necessary prerequisite for a successful work of art. Style, in his opinion, arose from a personal vision of the world and not, as Gauguin thought, purely from the imagination. He saw in the work of Gustave Courbet the confirmation of these beliefs. Courbet painted 'things [...] as they are'. Moreover, even now, Van Gogh remained true to 'the same ideas about colour' that he had had when he was 'in Holland', despite all the changes his art had undergone.

The visit Van Gogh and Gauguin paid to the Musée Fabre in Montpellier played an important role in their often stormy debates and further fired Van Gogh's love of Delacroix. In particular, the latter's portrait of Alfred Bruyas stuck in his mind. Van Gogh associated the figure with an unhappy man dressed in black in a poem by Alfred de Musset, and

The Grande Galerie of the Musée Fabre, Montpellier, c. 1904

his thoughts were full of this – in his opinion – extremely consoling work. The visit to the museum also served to shift Van Gogh's attention from brilliant colour effects towards the use of half-tones, of which Delacroix had been a master.

COLOUR AND LIGHT

Vincent van Gogh (1853-1890)
Head of a woman, 1885, Amsterdam,
Van Gogh Museum (Vincent van Gogh Foundation)

Peter Paul Rubens (1577-1640)
The carrying of the cross,
Amsterdam, Rijksmuseum

Peter Paul Rubens

Shortly after his visit to the Rijksmuseum in Amsterdam, which served to strengthen his interest in Rembrandt and Frans Hals, Van Gogh moved to Antwerp. During his time there he visited many churches and museums and made an exhaustive study of the work of Rubens. He also took lessons at the art academy. Although he painted only a handful of pictures in this period, he was now clearly in the process of leaving his dark Nuenen palette behind. In the Antwerp portraits, for example, he uses the lighter flesh tones employed by Rubens and his circle: 'In the woman's portrait I have brought lighter tones into the flesh, *white* tinted with carmine, vermilion, yellow and a light background of grey-yellow.'

Eugène Delacroix (1798-1863)
The barque of Dante (Dante and Virgil in hell), 1822,
Paris, Musée du Louvre

Eugène Delacroix (1798-1863)
Christ asleep during the tempest, c. 1853,
New York, The Metropolitan Museum of Art, Bequest of Mrs H.O. Havemeyer, 1929,
The H.O. Havemeyer Collection

Eugène Delacroix

Van Gogh often mentioned Delacroix in the same breath as Rembrandt. He felt particularly drawn to the French master because he, like Rembrandt, had been able to give great expression to his subjects.

Van Gogh had already become familiar with Delacroix's paintings in the early 1870s. While working in Nuenen in 1885, his enthusiasm for the Frenchman's technique was further kindled by reading about him. Following Delacroix's example, he began to construct his figures from large forms, reproducing the main masses of the body and only then drawing the contours. Van Gogh adopted this method in order to give his figures 'great expression'. However, although Delacroix's theories about drawing played an important role in Van Gogh's learning process, it was his use of colour – and particularly of colour contrasts – that made the deepest impression. His starting point was the idea that 'the mood *of the colours and the tone [be] at one with the meaning.*' For Delacroix, colour was the conveyer of mood.

When he encountered Delacroix's work again in Paris in 1886-88, Van Gogh was once more struck by his palette: 'Oh, what a beautiful painting that is by Eug. Delacroix, Christ in the boat on the Sea of Gennesaret! He – with his pale lemon-yellow aureole, sleeping, luminous in the dramatic purple, dark-blue, blood-red patch of the group of bewildered disciples – on that terrible emerald-green sea, rising, rising, right to the top of the frame.'

It was also in this period that Van Gogh first came into contact with the work of the impressionists and neo-impressionists, and this, too, formed a powerful stimulus to adapt his own style and colouring. A comparison of the way the impressionists and Delacroix used colour was, however, decided in the latter's favour. In August 1888 Van Gogh justified his preference in a letter to Theo: 'I shall not be very surprised if the impressionists soon find fault with my way of working, for it has been fertilised by Delacroix's ideas rather than theirs. Because instead

Vincent van Gogh (1853-1890)
Pietà (after Delacroix), 1889, Amsterdam,
Van Gogh Museum (Vincent van Gogh Foundation)

of trying to reproduce exactly what I have before my eyes, I use colour more arbitrarily, in order to express myself forcefully.'

Even in the south, Delacroix remained one of Van Gogh's great role models. Although in the last nine weeks of 1888 Van Gogh and Gauguin experimented with each other's style and palette, in neither case did these influences truly take root. In the period that followed, Van Gogh continued to revise and renew his colouring, brushstroke and technique, but only within the framework of possibilities he had explored in the previous years, and which, as an experienced artist, he had now fully mastered. In Delacroix he found the ideal palette for the kind of expressiveness he wished to give his paintings. The impressionists had never been interested in this sort of power of expression, almost symbolist in conception, so their work naturally offered Van Gogh no point of reference. Delacroix, on the other hand, provided him with the means to take modern art one step further.

Adolphe-Joseph Monticelli (1824-1886)
Vase with flowers, c. 1875, Amsterdam,
Van Gogh Museum (Vincent van Gogh Foundation)

Vincent van Gogh (1853-1890)
Vase with Chinese asters, 1886, Amsterdam,
Van Gogh Museum (Vincent van Gogh Foundation)

Adolphe-Joseph Monticelli (1824-1886)
Sunset, c. 1882-84,
London, The National Gallery

Adolphe-Joseph Monticelli

Around 1885-86 Van Gogh began to reject the palette of artists such as Israëls and Mauve, whose use of colour he had previously defended. He still had respect for these masters, but through the art of Delacroix, Hals, Rubens and the impressionists he came to a new understanding of colour and how it might be used. The work of the contemporary painter Adolphe Monticelli accorded well with his new views. Van Gogh admired how 'Monticelli sometimes made a bunch of flowers an excuse for gathering together in a single panel the whole range of his richest and most perfectly balanced tones,' claiming that 'you must go straight to Delacroix to find anything equal to his orchestration of colours.' Next to Delacroix, it was first and foremost Monticelli who had succeeded in capturing the essence of the Provençal landscape by means of colour. The southern French master's thick impasto also appealed to Van Gogh and served as a catalyst to further developments in his own brushwork.

Georges Seurat (1859-1891)
La Luzerne, Saint-Denis, 1885-86,
Edinburgh, National Galleries of Scotland

Georges Seurat (1859-1891)
*A Sunday afternoon on the island
of La Grande Jatte*, 1886,
The Art Institute of Chicago,
Helen Birch Bartlett Memorial Collection

Charles Angrand (1854-1926)
Feeding the chickens, 1884,
Copenhagen, Ny Carlsberg Glyptotek

Impressionism and post-impressionism

Although after his visit to the Rijksmuseum, his study of the work of Rubens in Antwerp and his readings on Delacroix Van Gogh had already begun to change his notion of colour, his own palette only became significantly brighter and more lively during his Paris period (1886-88), when he saw actual works by Delacroix and the impressionists.

Van Gogh regarded Claude Monet as a great renewer of landscape painting; Edgar Degas was to his mind the artist who had introduced the modern figure into art. 'In Antwerp I did not even know what the impressionists were, now I have seen them and though *not* being one of the club yet I have much admired certain impressionists' pictures – Degas nude figure – Claude Monet landscape,' he wrote. He also thought highly of Camille Pissarro, the only impressionist to have taken rural labour as his subject. However, although Van Gogh admired the luminous works of Monet, Pissarro and Renoir, in terms of both style and content he himself was in search of something different.

In Paris, Van Gogh met a group of young progressive artists who considered impressionism too subjective and too focused on achieving purely visual effects. Like them, Vincent wanted to represent more than merely his own sensation of the landscape, captured using a bright palette and fleeting brushwork. His new circle enthusiastically greeted Georges Seurat's enormous *Sunday afternoon on the island of La Grande Jatte*, exhibited at the Salon des Indépendants in the spring of 1886, regarding it as the manifesto of an entirely new style. Van Gogh had only just arrived in Paris at the time of the show and still had much to see and learn; it was not until many months later that he actually began to consider neo-impressionism in any serious way.

In the spring of 1887 Van Gogh went painting with Paul Signac in the suburbs of Paris. Once Signac had taught him the principles of neo-impressionism, Van Gogh began experimenting with his own variation on the pointillist touch – for example in *Courting couples in the Voyer*

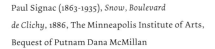

d'Argenson Park in Asnières, an homage both to the *fêtes galantes* of Watteau and to Seurat's *Grande Jatte*.

He also went on painting excursions with his young friend Emile Bernard. Bernard also explored neo-impressionism but rejected its precepts fairly quickly. He was more fascinated by the use of pure colour and simplified forms. His experiments in this direction would prove important for Van Gogh's further development.

Henri de Toulouse-Lautrec shared Van Gogh's enthusiasm for illustration, caricature and Japanese prints. He drew his motifs mainly from the world of cabarets and Paris nightlife. Although this milieu attracted Bernard, who soon began to adopt it as his own, apart from a few café and restaurant scenes Van Gogh preferred to seek his subject matter in the open air. Like Bernard and Louis Anquetin, Toulouse-Lautrec also worked for a brief period in the neo-impressionist manner. Closest to the style is undoubtedly his *Young woman at a table, 'Poudre de riz'*. Van Gogh was deeply impressed by the picture, and Theo acquired it for their joint collection.

Henri de Toulouse-Lautrec (1864-1901)
Young woman at a table, 'Poudre de riz', 1887,
Amsterdam, Van Gogh Museum
(Vincent van Gogh Foundation)

Vincent van Gogh (1853-1890)
Courting couples in the Voyer d'Argenson Park in Asnières, 1887,
Amsterdam, Van Gogh Museum (Vincent van Gogh Foundation)

Louis Anquetin (1861-1932), *Avenue de Clichy*,
1887, Hartford, Wadsworth Atheneum
Museum of Art, The Ella Gallup Sumner
and Mary Catlin Sumner Collection Fund

Vincent van Gogh (1853-1890)
Café terrace at night, 1888,
Otterlo, Kröller-Müller Museum

Vincent van Gogh (1853-1890)
Portrait of Père Tanguy, half-length, 1887,
Paris, Musée Rodin

left:
Vincent van Gogh (1853-1890)
Still life with coffeepot, 1888,
private collection

Emile Bernard (1868-1941)
The blue coffeepot, 1888,
Kunsthalle Bremen

Vincent van Gogh (1853-1890)
Still life with quinces and lemons, 1887,
Amsterdam, Van Gogh Museum (Vincent van Gogh Foundation)

In November 1887 Van Gogh organised an exhibition of works by his artist-friends at a restaurant on the Avenue de Clichy, and it was on this occasion that he coined the term 'impressionists of the Petit Boulevard'. Together with Bernard, Anquetin, Toulouse-Lautrec and the young Dutchman Koning, he displayed a large number of works, which drew the attention of other members of the avant-garde.

Van Gogh's sojourn in Paris was invaluable for the evolution of his art. Both the older generation of impressionists and the avant-garde – Angrand, Anquetin, Bernard, Gauguin, Seurat and Signac – left their mark on his painting, as did the powerful contrasting colour fields of the Japanese printmakers. All these various influences led to the new, more colourful palette and varied brushstroke of Van Gogh's later work.

PRINTS

Vincent Van Gogh (1853-1890)
Letter 395/330 to Theo van Gogh, Nieuw-Amsterdam,
probably 2 October 1883, Amsterdam,
Van Gogh Museum (Vincent van Gogh Foundation)

After Hubert von Herkomer (1849-1914)
Sunday at Chelsea Hospital, 1875,
Amsterdam, Van Gogh Museum
(Vincent van Gogh Foundation)

After Percy T. Macquoid (1852-1925)
The mackerel fishery – sketches in a Devonshire village, 1874,
Amsterdam, Van Gogh Museum (Vincent van Gogh Foundation)

Artists never work in a vacuum. Those privileged with a glimpse into the artist's studio will frequently find reproductions scattered about or hanging on the walls, sometimes seemingly carelessly stuck up with pins. Such images can serve as inspiration, motivation, or even a form of consolation. There are numerous examples of artworks in which other paintings or prints have left their trace – and this is certainly true in the oeuvre of Vincent van Gogh. It is almost impossible to overestimate the importance of the graphic arts in his development. A visitor to his Nuenen studio remembered that there were 'drawings, studies, illustrations everywhere – especially from *The Graphic* – to the left and right on the floor, on chairs – a real mess.' Van Gogh undoubtedly spent many hours cutting up magazines and arranging them in portfolios. Prints were useful to him in several ways: they not only answered to his aesthetic sense but also provided him with information of a formal nature, for example, on the power of contour lines or how to design a composition or create mood. They were thus an important stimulus to his own work. The entire gamut of his tastes and interests are represented in the collection.

After Honoré Daumier (1808-1879), *The four ages of a drinker*, 1862,
Amsterdam, Van Gogh Museum (Vincent van Gogh Foundation)

Vincent van Gogh (1853-1890)
Small pear tree in blossom, 1888,
Amsterdam, Van Gogh Museum
(Vincent van Gogh Foundation)

tagawa Hiroshige (1797-1858)
udden shower on the Great Bridge near Atake,
57, Amsterdam, Van Gogh Museum
Vincent van Gogh Foundation)

Vincent van Gogh (1853-1890)
Bridge in the rain (after Hiroshige), 1887,
Amsterdam, Van Gogh Museum
(Vincent van Gogh Foundation)

Utagawa Hiroshige (1797-1858)
The plum tree teahouse at Kameido, 1857,
Amsterdam, Van Gogh Museum
(Vincent van Gogh Foundation)

From the moment he discovered them, in Antwerp in 1886, Japanese prints intrigued Van Gogh. He became a passionate collector of these woodblock prints, particularly during his sojourn in Paris. Together with Theo, he acquired hundreds of sheets, among them many so-called *ukiyo-e* prints, 'visions of the floating world'. Kunisada is well represented, and there are a number of pieces by Kuniyoshi and Hiroshige, many depicting Japanese nightlife, courtesans, bordellos or theatre performances. What appealed to Van Gogh in these works were the bright (often primary) colours, the daring compositions with the unexpected croppings and aerial perspective, the powerful contours, the decorative patterns and novel, non-western motifs. His desire to work in the Japanese manner resulted in a painting style characterised by brilliant fields of colour and asymmetrical, clipped compositions. His enthusiasm for these *Japanoiseries* left other traces as well – for example in his increasing interest in irises, blossoms of all kinds, panoramic landscapes and in delineating his figures with only a few 'characteristic strokes'. He also made painted copies after a number of the prints in his collection.

Van Gogh's fascination did not end with the creation of works in the spirit of his Japanese counterparts, for, as with Millet and Delacroix, these exotic idols were role models for life itself. He believed they had lived a sober and fraternal existence, in complete harmony with nature, 'as if they were flowers themselves'. Reading articles and books about Japan further fostered this utopian image. The plan to found an artists' colony in Arles was partly inspired by his conviction that the Japanese artists had themselves once realised the same ideal. Although he failed in his endeavour, he did convince Bernard, Gauguin and Charles Laval to create self-portraits on the Japanese model and to exchange them amongst themselves as tokens of friendship.

VAN GOGH'S MUSÉE RÉALISÉ

Paul Gauguin (1848-1903), *Self-portrait with portrait of Bernard, 'Les misérables'*, 1888,
Amsterdam, Van Gogh Museum (Vincent van Gogh Foundation)

Emile Bernard (1868-1941)
Self-portrait with portrait of Gauguin, 1888,
Amsterdam, Van Gogh Museum (Vincent van Gogh Foundation)

While in Paris, Van Gogh conceived the idea of forming an artists' group, to be made up of himself and a number of other avant-garde painters. In 1887 he organised an exhibition of the work of these fellow-artists, dubbing them the 'impressionists of the Petit Boulevard' – as a contrast to the established and successful impressionists of the 'Grand Boulevard'.

In Arles he once again took up the notion of founding a kind of community of kindred spirits. He rented the Yellow House, anticipating that his friends from Paris would eventually join him in his 'studio of the south'. In particular, he wanted Gauguin to come. Gauguin did, but the dream of a painters' collective was never realised. Nonetheless, Van Gogh did manage to set up a kind of symbolic cooperative by asking several artists to exchange their self-portraits with him. In October 1888 he received the likenesses of Bernard and Gauguin. Charles Laval, a friend of the latter made a contribution as well: 'You will also be pleased to hear that we have an addition to the collection of portraits of artists. The self-portrait by Laval, extremely good,' Vincent wrote to Theo. In addition, while in Arles, Gauguin executed his *Portrait of Van Gogh*

Charles Laval (1862-1894), *Self-portrait*, 1888,
Amsterdam, Van Gogh Museum (Vincent van Gogh Foundation)

Paul Gauguin (1848-1903)

Portrait of Van Gogh painting sunflowers, 1888,

Amsterdam, Van Gogh Museum (Vincent van Gogh Foundation)

painting sunflowers. 'Have you seen that portrait he did of me painting sunflowers? My face has certainly brightened up since then, but it was really me, extremely tired and charged with electricity as I was then.' Thus developed Van Gogh's small portrait gallery of like-minded painters, today in the Van Gogh Museum. Together with his own copies after such favourite masters as Delacroix, Hiroshige, Millet and Rembrandt, they make up the artist's own personal *musée réalisé*.

GRANDMAS from MARS

Words by

Michelle Robinson

BLOOMSBURY
LONDON OXFORD NEW YORK NEW DELHI SYDNEY

Illustrations by

Fred Blunt

Fred and Nell's parents are off to a meeting.
But first they tell Grandma,

"Here's what they'll be eating.

It's school in the morning,
they can't be up late...